THIS BOO

GW00706042

....

THE WORLD'S MOST DELIGHTFUL/
UGLY/CHARMING/SEXY/CRUDE/
BORING/CUTE/STUPID/CANCERIAN

BEST WISHES FROM/YOURS IN DISGUST
ALL MY LOVE......................

P.S. PLEASE TAKE NOTE OF PAGE(S)

....

Ian Heath's Cancer Book

ISBN 1-905134-06-1

Published by Ian Heath Books
9 Adam Street
The Strand
London WC2N 6AA

www.ianheathart.com

Ian heath's CANCER BOOK

CANCER

JUNE 21 – JULY 20

FOURTH SIGN OF THE ZODIAC
SYMBOL : THE CRAB
RULING PLANET : THE MOON
COLOURS : WHITE, SEA-GREEN
GEMS : PEARL, AQUAMARINE
NUMBER : TWO
DAY : MONDAY
METAL : SILVER
FLOWER : MAGNOLIA

..... KNOWS HIS/HER VALUE............

.... IS PIG-HEADED...............

... CLIMBS TO TOP OF THE LADDER ....

.... CAN BE OLD-FASHIONED........

.......IS A WORRIER.................

..... KNOWS WHAT PEOPLE WANT......

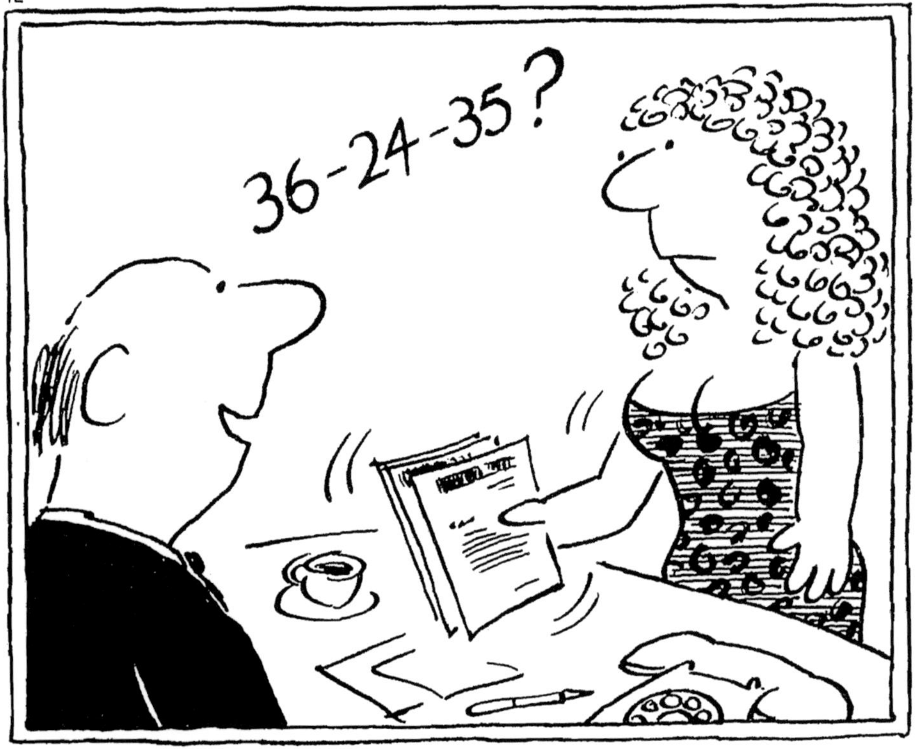

.....IS GOOD AT FIGURES.........

..... FAIRLY AGGRESSIVE ....

.... RATHER SHY................

.... AND DOESN'T PANIC.

...... AN ARCHAEOLOGIST...........

..... RIDING INSTRUCTOR ....

...... SHIP'S CAPTAIN............

.... GARDENER ....

.... WAITRESS ....

...MARRIAGE COUNSELLOR.........

.... OR BANK-MANAGER.

The
CANCERIAN
at home............

.... IS A HOARDER ....

.......LIKES TO BE WARM..........

.......IS VIDEO-CRAZY.............

..........ABSENT-MINDED...........

.........VERY STRICT..............

.....ENJOYS WALKING THE DOG.........

.... WINE-MAKING...............

.......LOVES WORD GAMES..........

.... READING LONG NOVELS ....

......AND LIKES SILENCE.

.... BALLROOM DANCING ....

..........FAST CARS..................

...... COLLECTING BUTTERFLIES.........

.... HORSE–RIDING ....

.........BUBBLE-BATHS...............

... AND BUBBLE-GUM.

. . . . SNAKES . . . .

.... SOAP-OPERAS ....

.......NOISY CHILDREN.............

...... INCOME TAX DEMANDS ....

.... KEEPING FIT.................

...... AND GARLIC.

...... HAS HIGH STANDARDS.........

... DOESN'T LIKE MAKE-UP..........

..... WON'T LET GO...............

.... IS TENDER ....

.....CAN BE TEARFUL...........

.... CONCEALS PASSION..........

.... LAUGHS A LOT..............

.....IS YOUNG—AT—HEART............

...HAS TO TELL THE WORLD...........

.... AND IS SHY.

CANCERIAN AND PARTNER

HEART RATINGS

♥♥♥♥♥ WOWEE!!

♥♥♥♥ GREAT, BUT NOT 'IT'

♥♥♥ O.K. – COULD BE FUN

♥♥ FORGET IT

♥ WALK QUICKLY THE OTHER WAY

SCORPIO   PISCES

LEO VIRGO GEMINI
TAURUS

ARIES CANCER

LIBRA CAPRICORN

SAGITTARIUS AQUARIUS

CANCER PEOPLE

HARRISON FORD · EDGAR DEGAS
NATALIE WOOD · PIERRE CARDIN
CARLOS SANTANA · TOM HANKS
KEN RUSSELL · GIORGIO ARMANI
NELSON MANDELA · RINGO STARR

MERYL STREEP · GEORGE ORWELL
GEORGE MICHAEL · MEL BROOKS
LOUIS ARMSTRONG · NEIL SIMON
TOM CRUISE · PAMELA ANDERSON
COURTNEY LOVE · JEAN COCTEAU
SYLVESTER STALLONE · LIV TYLER
GEORGE W BUSH · REMBRANDT
DAVID HOCKNEY · BILL HALEY
PRINCESS DIANA · DALAI LAMA
JEFF BECK · RICHARD BRANSON
GEORGIE FAME · JULIUS CAESER